For Will. You will never truly understand what an inspiration you've been to me over the last few years. Your bravery, honesty, gratitude and resilience are a model. This book and many others have been floating around in my head for many years but without your example, it wouldn't have happened.

For Jess. The best outbound BDR on the planet. You define what it is to be a fantastic human being, an incredible parent, a wonderful daughter and the very definition of BDR 2.0. No one is better.

THE ANATOMY OF YOUR FIRST SALES PLAYBOOK

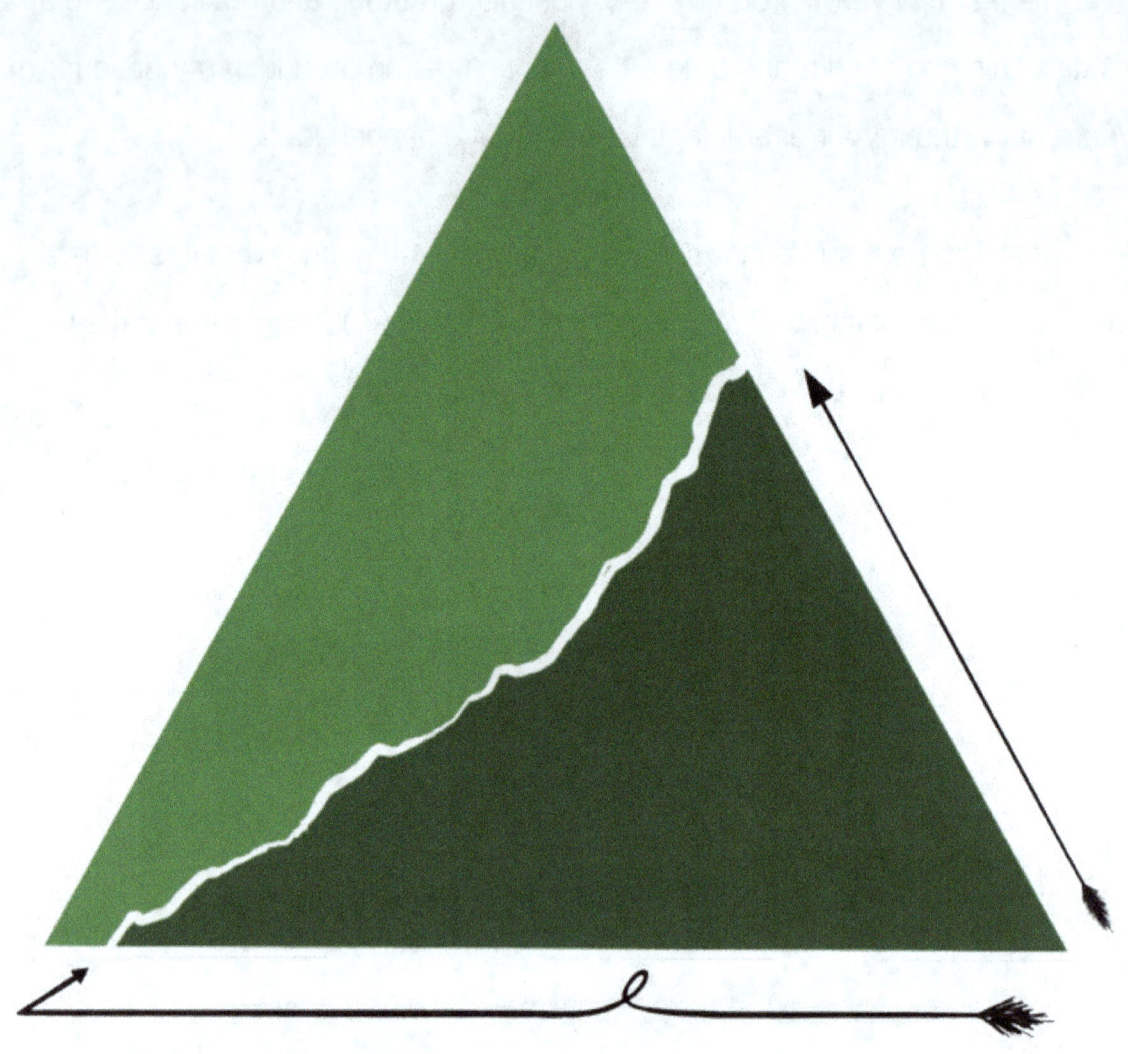

James Moss

How to use this book

First, read it. Then use the Sales Process Outline in the Appendix while referring back to the content as appropriate. I can email you the deck in .ppt or slides if you'd like. If you already work for a big company, but are reading this book, please send me an email. Your basic steps are the same, but there is a ton more complexity with a company that is already large. You need this, but you also need some additional customization.

This is exactly the same process that I follow with my clients that are under $5 million/year in sales. If you get stuck, have a question, or any feedback; send me a note: jmoss@inertiasolutions.io

Let's start with some background. Over the last 30 years, I am grateful to have been able to lead, build, and scale successful and unsuccessful sales organizations in several industries and I've consulted in many more. Over that time, I grew to love sales process, sales psychology, leadership, training and working with wonderful human beings. So, it is due time to pass on what I've learned. My true passion lies with entrepreneurs. Those brave souls with a solution to a problem that just LEAP and hope that a net appears. I truly hope that this short book is one of those nets. If I can help you in any way, just reach out. My business is, well, busy, but it is also one of my hobbies. If I can help, I will certainly try.

This isn't going to be easy, but you can do it if you follow the steps. You have to do some hard, introspective work but, the process itself is simple. Let's start out with a couple of "reasons why". You can feel free to skip to Part 3 if you are chomping at the bit to get rolling with the technical details. However, if you ever wonder why you are on the journey, see if you can relate to Parts 1 and 2. As a point of interest, there is an old idea that all sales books have the best content in the first four chapters, then the rest just justifies the good stuff and the twenty bucks you spent. That's not the case here. I hate fluff. Let's go!

PART 1: THE WORKED ONCE FALLACY

As leaders, how many times have we seen a new employee have early success and then sputter out just a few weeks later? They looked like they were working hard and it was seemingly obvious that they knew what they were doing. So, why is the "sophomore slump" so prevalent in sales?

Early in my selling career, I went to work as an AE for a company that offered instructor lead computer software training. I had a little bit of sales experience and a lot of ambition. In my first month, I shattered their long standing month one sales record by more than double. My ego was so big that I had to go through the double doors out front lest my inflated head not fit.

The comp plan at this company allowed AEs to decide between a "base plus" model and a 100% commission model that, if worked properly, yielded much more cash. The catch was that you couldn't go back to the "base plus" model once you had made the leap.

Needless to say, I jumped at the commission plan after my first month because I obviously had this thing figured out. Not inconsequentially, my young family also needed the money.

A hard lesson came in month two. I sold NOTHING. Zip. Zero. No paycheck. If it wasn't for my exceptional results in month one, I would have been fired on the spot.

My boss, Ron (Hey, Ron!), sat me down and went over my methodology. His diagnosis was spot on. Our company had a well documented process and I simply wasn't using it. If it was school, an "F" would have been too generous.

Of course, because of my early success, I protested. "Ron, buddy, look at all I sold last month. I'm, doing exactly the same thing!"

Now, Ron is an analytical guy, but he didn't have any answers beyond, "follow the process, Jim". So, with deep scars and an empty stomach, I started over. Eventually, I was able to get back to the top of the stack rankings but, along the way, I saw many others that weren't as fortunate. They either quit or were let go. In a team of over twenty reps, I was third in seniority after one year. YIKES.

Years later, I wanted my employees to avoid this pitfall so I analyzed my own behavior. It turns out that, in month one, I was so enthusiastic about my new job that I could have said just about anything and still sold a ton of courses. Much like a new entrepreneur, people loved talking to me because I was happy, excited, and confident. My words and/or skills mattered much less than how I was behaving. That kind of blind ambition only lasts so long and the default process takes over.

After the honeymoon was over and the excitement waned, my aimless wanderings outside of the process stopped working. It was truly terrifying. In fact, it was like a bad horror movie. No matter which door I opened, there was a wall of chainsaws cutting my pitch to bits.

So, an enthusiastic new sales rep will typically have success, but a great sales leader will make sure to inspect that work to ensure that it falls inside of the proven sales process so that their foundations are set for long term success. Just because it worked once . . . Sound familiar? I watched this play out, almost helplessly, for many years as a sales leader until, finally, the way to (mostly) avert the dreaded sophomore slump was revealed.

PART 2: PROCESS, NO PROCESS

Your brand new company is thriving. You, the founder, are still taking most every sales call. It is almost easy, but it is time to hand the reigns to a sales pro so you can get back to leading the culture and the product push to elevate your enterprise even further.

You hire a sales person. She tells you she has a process. She thrives and makes it past the "Worked Once Fallacy". Then she hits a wall. You think that is just a natural capacity issue so you hire another sales person. Same result. But you were selling twice as much. Your competitor's reps are doing even better than that! WHY?

Every decent sales person has a default process. Most of them are opportunists. They understand sales goals very well, but they still most always gravitate to working with deals that are closer to the end of the sales cycle. We are kind of like children. Disneyland is a closed deal. Prospecting is doing your chores. Documentation is that dirty dish we hid in the nightstand.

For me, I always scoured the CRM for the lowest hanging fruit. In a small company, where I was the only or one of few sales people, I could make a decent living for some time doing this. My pitch was better (because of a ton of sales technique training) so I could close deals that others had lost. Problem: I hated prospecting. I'd do it when I had to, but my passion and skill were at the end of the sales process, not the beginning. So, my tendency was to focus on the opportunities that I had, not the ones that I needed. As it turns out, I was NOT alone.

So, sales ride a rollercoaster. Good months (deal closing months) and bad months (frantic prospecting months). Up. Down. Up. Down. Like an oil derrick in West Texas but slower and more painful to watch.

Over 85% of the companies that I interview have no formal sales process, no real sales leadership, no KPIs beyond the top line and no sales training plan. Zip. Nada. Nothing. You can have the best product in the world, but if you don't plan for success, it very likely won't come to find you. Treat sales like the critical profession that it is, complete with planning and leadership and, suddenly, every day is Disneyland.

This isn't limited to small, founder lead organizations. I've worked with companies that have grown at half speed for years before they realized that sales process is as critical as any other process in their business. It is actually quite shocking.

PARTS 3 and 4: BUILDING YOUR PLAYBOOK

Now that we've firmly established the need for a formal sales process, lets jump right in. For the first 15 years (out of 29 so far) of my sales career, there was no formal process. Let that sink in. 14 years ago, I was asked to document what my team was doing to provide insight for a potential merger. The first domino dropped to what has become my passion.

First off, the process has to be specific to your vision. Sounds simple. But, let's make sure you have an actionable vision first.

Format: I like do present the plan in a deck (PowerPoint, Slides, etc.) with each concept on its own page(s). This way, it can easily be chopped up into sections to be shared with the appropriate people and, when the time comes, it can be presented as a whole to investors, new execs, board members, etc.

Before you move on, set up the deck so you can start aggregating your thoughts as you read. If you are like me, you might forget a key point. Remember, there is a sample in the appendix. As stated earlier, I can send you a copy in Slides or PowerPoint. jmoss@inertiasolutions.io

Part 3A: Your Vision, Mission, Values and Leadership Brand

Your vision should be an aspirational statement of what your company will become. This statement should be the litmus test for every decision made within the organization. Once you have this battle cry, you can take the next steps. This is NECESSARY even if you are a sole proprietor. You may already have one, but can it pass the litmus test above? If not, read on. If so, skip to Part 3B.

Creating a vision should be a fairly straightforward idea, but many leaders are paralyzed by it. It is akin to answering the "what do you want to be when you grow up?" question for your business. However, it doesn't have to be that hard. Because the vision is aspirational and achievable, it can be changed. It just has to be challenging, possible, and contain your desired future state. You should be able to "see it". If you are an OKR fan, it is the O for the whole company.

Start with "To Become . . . " and fill in the blanks. It should be specific enough to understand, but subjective enough that you don't get caught on a technicality. It should be obvious when you achieve it. It should be inspirational.

Examples:

"To become the most well known pet care brand in North Carolina."

"To become the fastest growing widget alignment software company in the English speaking world."

"To become the company that sells the most flea collars online in a calendar year."

This MUST be done. I'm inflexible here. Marketers and branders will automatically do this as part of a brand study, but it is so much more than that. It is the foundational element that the entire company is built on. How can a sales team operate without it?

If it doesn't support the vision, we don't do it. The vision is YOU when you aren't available. Read that again.

Your company should already have a mission and values. If not, let me know, I can help. You can even create mission and values just for the sales team.

On the other hand, not many companies have published their leadership brand. Leadership brand can be defined as the 3 or 4 tenets that demonstrate "how we act". For example.

Courage and Candor with Kindness: We always tell the truth but we do it in a way that is both brave and kind. Our goal is to inform not to belittle or downplay.

We seek and value Feedback. All truthful feedback is valued, even if it is perceived as being negative. There is always a lesson to be learned.

We embrace Failure as an Opportunity to Learn. We are pioneers. As such, we understand that we will have setbacks. We celebrate them as opportunities to to get better every day.

We are Agile. Instead of lamenting over our circumstances when they don't fit our vision, we change them. We take the appropriate risks for each situation. We analyze quickly, get 75% of the information and GO.

Again, just examples. Leadership brand should be universal within the company and realized in practice, not aspirational like vision.

Now on to the detail. The devil, as it were . . .

Part 3B: The Customer

Who is your customer? Specifically! Take the time to deeply understand who actually buys from you. It isn't, "who we want to buy from us." It is, "who buys from us today?"

I find it helpful to build a formal Ideal Customer Profile (ICP) and specific buyer personas.

This is important because we can use them to determine how your buyer likes to buy and how they like to be sold to. Simple, right? Trouble here is that it requires some introspection that may provide some truths that you weren't prepared for. Founders push back here all the time. I just shrug. Data doesn't lie. These are your people (for now). Your customer facing team MUST know who they are dealing with inside and out. Don't assume anything.

Ideal Customer Profile: There are quite a few ways to define this. My preference is that we focus on the reasons the customer is aligned with your product.

Where are they located?

Are they a business or an individual? If business, how big and what type?

Who is the decisionmaker? (CEO, head of household, teenager, operations manager, etc.)

What problems do they have that we can solve?

Where do they congregate?

Head to your deck and document all of that.

Buyer Personas: Here we define the ICP as a Human Being.

What is their name? Their gender, age, ethnicity, income, how many kids? Managerial level?

What types of things to they purchase? Where do they purchase them?

What keeps them awake at night? What excites them? How do they like their coffee?

AND every other attribute you can apply.

When you inspect this in your current customer base, you will likely find that you have more than one buyer persona. Maybe you'll have as many as 3. Document all of them in the playbook.

Example: If you sell Widget Manufacturing Operations Software, one of your buyer personas could look like this:

Name: Sara Operations

Age: 35-55

Gender: Female

Education: Bachelor's degree or higher in engineering, operations management, or related field

Job Title: Operations Manager, Production Manager, Plant Manager, or similar

Industry: Manufacturing (specifically widget manufacturing)

Company Size: Mid-sized to large manufacturing company

Motivations: Improve operational efficiency and productivity. Streamline manufacturing processes. Reduce costs associated with production. Enhance quality control and ensure product consistency.

Pain Points: Inefficient production processes leading to delays and bottlenecks. Difficulty in tracking and managing inventory.

Lack of real-time visibility into manufacturing operations. Compliance issues with industry regulations.

Goals: Increase output without sacrificing quality. Implement automation and digitization within the manufacturing process. Optimize resource utilization to reduce waste. Stay competitive in the market by adopting modern technologies.

Behavioral Information: Researches extensively before making purchasing decisions. Prefers software solutions that offer customizable features to fit specific manufacturing needs. Values long-term relationships with software providers and seeks ongoing support and updates. Relies on peer recommendations and industry forums for evaluating software options.

Tech: Utilizes enterprise resource planning (ERP) systems or manufacturing execution systems (MES) for managing operations. Familiar with Industry 4.0 technologies and trends such as Internet of Things (IoT), big data analytics, and cloud computing. Comfortable with adopting new software solutions to enhance manufacturing capabilities.

Communication Preferences: Prefers email communication for initial outreach and information sharing. Open to scheduling demonstrations or webinars to explore software functionalities. Appreciates personalized communication that addresses specific pain points and concerns. Hasn't answered her phone since 2004.

WHEW, that is A LOT! Take the time, look at your current customers. If you don't have customers, look at the customers of your closest competitor. If those don't exist, start with the target you believe will be the closest and adjust the personas as data becomes available.

Value Drivers

Why do people actually buy your product? What are the 2 to 4 needs that are paid off when they become long term customers?

Do they save time?

Do they make more money?

Are they happier?

Are their customers happier?

Be very specific and very much entrenched in the feedback you have from your current customers, not what you think they might have wanted. Removing personal bias in this part of the process is absolutely critical. It is dangerous to assume you know anything until your customers tell you in their own words.

Bonus: If you ask your customers why they buy, you'll get some juicy customer stories for your sales process and for marketing to highlight on the website.

Part 3C: Leads and Prospecting

First things first, You'll need to document a few things before the first email is sent or phone call is made (based on the preference specified in your buyer personas). How do you keep track of ALL communications? If you are just starting out, consider signing up for a CRM that includes a sequencing tool. There are quite a few. I personally use Hubspot (2024), but the choice is yours.

Now, What does your messaging look like? You'll need compelling content for your prospecting communications that is thoroughly A/B tested on an ongoing basis. AI can help here, but there needs to be some level of personalization and specialization based on lead source. Put an outline of the various sequences (I define this downstream a little) that you will use in the playbook. Have a separate place to store the actual content; likely inside the CRM or engagement platform (if you have one). Lastly, clearly define a goal for outreach. What does success look like? USUALLY, it is one of two things. For a transactional product, the goal is a sale. For a product that requires more consultation, the goal is a discovery call, demo, or consultation. These are KPIs that need to be documented at this stage. Remember, again, that this is all dynamic and needs to change in real time as lessons are learned.

Who manages prospecting? Is it marketing? Is it sales? Is it its own thing (BDR/SDR team)? For now, we are going to assume that your sales rep(s) are responsible. Consider the following. The process is dynamic and you can move the responsibility later. When you start to move the needle, I like prospecting to be its own function with its own KPIs. Reason: I am personally a really good closer but a terrible opener. It seems to be almost universal. When one person is responsible for both ends of the process, they will gravitate to what they are the best at. You need it ALL.

Please understand that the ideal of sales development as its own function has undergone a ton of scrutiny as the future unfolds. I've been doing a ton of research and iteration lately on this topic and comparing it to my own experience leading evolving sales teams over the last few years.

The gurus on LinkedIn are screaming from the rooftops about how the SDR (Sales Development Rep) role is dead and that AI + automation is bringing back the "full stack" AE.   Maybe. Maybe (probably) not.

 So, let's address the gurus first. You know the ones. They had some early success in something and now work for a big company as the CXO or SVP of all that is good. Now, they are really good at social media and, very likely, their day job as a senior leader at BigCo.com. Does that have anything to do with us? Well, kinda.

The idea that is being propagated is that the SDR role is something that can be automated with intelligent, AI-created dynamic messaging along with automation tools that run the process. This can either be owned by the AE responsible for that group of prospects/territory or by marketing. Sounds good. Could work. But, is there room for a role LIKE an SDR? YES!

The reason is very simple. Marketing, Prospecting, and Selling all have interrelated but different skillsets. As such, they have different KPIs. For simplicity's sake: 1. Marketers generate interest (MQLs) 2. SDRs filter the interest and get people in to initial meetings 3. AEs find alignment and guide prospects through sales process.

Can automation and AI replace the SDR? To a certain extent, yes. However, there is a special skillset that is needed to really nail this conversion point. Someone has to be responsible for the sequences, for A/B testing, for ensuring the AI is nailing messaging, and, ultimately, for the number of qualified prospects that land on AE calendars. Meet SDR2.0!

This person is VASTLY different from the turn and burn SDR of 2016.

In fact, they can replace several "old school" SDRs.

They are expert writers, expert SDR-Ops pros, expert ICP filters and, yes, they can still pick up the phone to make sure that an engager shows up to their demo!

Can a sales rep/AE do this? Sure. What about Marketing? Yep. Both of those are great stop gaps if you can't afford to specialize your team just yet, but don't get starry eyed over AI replacing the SDR role or its KPIs just yet. The real live person with the responsibility of keeping AE calendars full is an evolved professional with singular purpose that is more necessary now than ever. AI and automation are tools to be used by professionals, NOT replace them (not the smart ones anyway).

So, is the SDR dead? Well, the ones that haven't evolved should brush up on their skills.

Next, there are four ways to get leads.

They are as follows: Advertising (SEM, social ads, postcards, smoke signals, etc.), Content (thought leadership, blogs, webinars, SEO and so on), Outreach and Referrals. That's it. What's your mix today and how does each type impact CAC (probably a question for marketing, but I'm happy to chat about it)?

Advertising: This is typically the most expensive way to get leads. The methodology should be well documented in your marketing plan. From the sales perspective, this is a moving target and should be revalued constantly. The KPI here is Cost Per Lead (CPL) v. Revenue Per Lead (RPL). Sometimes paid advertising is just so expensive that it doesn't make sense. Other times, it is amazing. I consider tradeshows and webinars to also be in this category. Of course, grey area abounds because you are also providing content in those venues.

Two Stories:

I worked with a company that spent $500,000 on a paid advertising engine over 4 months. It resulted in one $8,000 sale valued at less that $50,000 over its lifetime. That was a BAD investment.

Another company in my portfolio had a $1200/month ad spend limit that resulted in over $100,000/month in revenue. On the surface, it looks like they should have spent more, but above that number there were 2 issues. First, the lead quality went down and, second, they were onboarding staff just fast enough to support the spend. It was a GREAT investment.

I am not a marketer, but advertising should be tested by your demand generation/marketing team on a "low risk" basis. Double down when it works, throttle back when it doesn't. Give your marketing department KPIs like number of opportunities sourced from marketing qualified leads and over/under budget. Not just raw number of leads, but leads that actually go somewhere.

Content: We are assuming you have a website. If not, you should build one. If you are savvy enough to start a business, you can build a simple website that can be rebuilt once revenue starts rolling in.

The main type of content that I focus on from the sales side falls under "thought leadership". You are obviously an expert in your field. Your website should highlight that expertise by providing as much knowledge as possible to the world for free without crossing into your paid product (too much). Your sales plan may not have a section for content strategy, but these types of leads need to be addressed specifically. They have their own messaging per category.

This can be blogs, vlogs (with transcripts), white papers or anything else that adds value to your industry.

It takes time, but if you are genuine and don't try to get cute with the Google algorithm, the leads that come from content will be some of your best. If you really know your stuff and are active online, people will opt in and ask for your help/product/service/knowledge. This is hard and takes a good marketer, but these are great leads. This type of lead generation is out of scope for the sales playbook, but we need to know how many of them are in the mix now and in the future. They simply close at a much higher rate than anything except referrals.

Outreach: Cold calling is dead, long live outreach. In today's climate, I would never suggest making shotgun style cold calls. People are just immune and it is rude. However, we have some really good definitions for our ICP and buyer personas. It absolutely makes sense to reach out to them with some degree of personalization. What does that look like? If this isn't something you've done before, there are a couple of good rules of thumb.

Stick to value. Don't try to be clever. Again, people have become immune to old school sales tactics.

Be brief. A sentence along with two or three bullets is enough

Be personal. Find common ground or something about the lead that is genuinely compelling. Also, tell your story (briefly). Be a human.

Be specific. What problems can you solve and what do you expect as a call to action? Reach out with purpose.

Average sales people give up after two contact attempts. You need to catch someone when they are in the right head space. That could take seven or eight, polite, value driven attempts over a period of weeks.

When someone finally engages, don't make them wait.

If a prospect responds, visits your website or even has a positive thought about your offering, pick up the phone. RIGHT NOW. You have to be relentless in communications when a prospect goes into shopping mode. The more responsive you are, the higher chances you have of success. Document all of this in the playbook. What are your standards? Mine is 5 minutes or less during business hours.

Bonus: Your very best source of cold outreach will come from a sequence that I call: Qualified, Bad Timing. Pretty self explanatory? These are people that respond by stating that they have interest, but the timing is bad. Our rep asks them for a better date, then trigger the above sequence on that date.

Referrals: Again, you want them. Always ask for them at the right time (when a prospect or customer is happy). They are fantastic. However, we are going to ignore them in all of our calculations. That said, referrals should be treated in much the same way as a content lead. They have expressed interest at the highest level and need to be communicated with accordingly. A couple of things to put in the plan: Referrals get the white glove treatment and referrals pay retail (everybody pays retail).

Now that you understand your audience , we need to determine what they are interested in, where they congregate, and who (as in their names) they are. We also need to know how effective your marketing engine is versus how many leads you need to create the sales velocity that will ultimately help you achieve your vision. So, do some math. How many leads does it take? Then make a specific plan based on your situation to get them in the door. This plan is obviously marketing heavy, and marketing needs to commit, but it is important that we use brutally honest data that we can see with our own eyes today.

Sequences: What is a sequence? A sequence, for the purposes of creating a playbook, is a series of semi-custom communications designed to get a lead to engage with you and/or your team. Sequences are used by all lead types and the messaging is specific to both the source and the individual. It wouldn't make a lot of sense to call a lead one time and then forget they exist, would it? Sounds silly, but all of us have done it.

It could look like this (just one sample, you'll need a few):

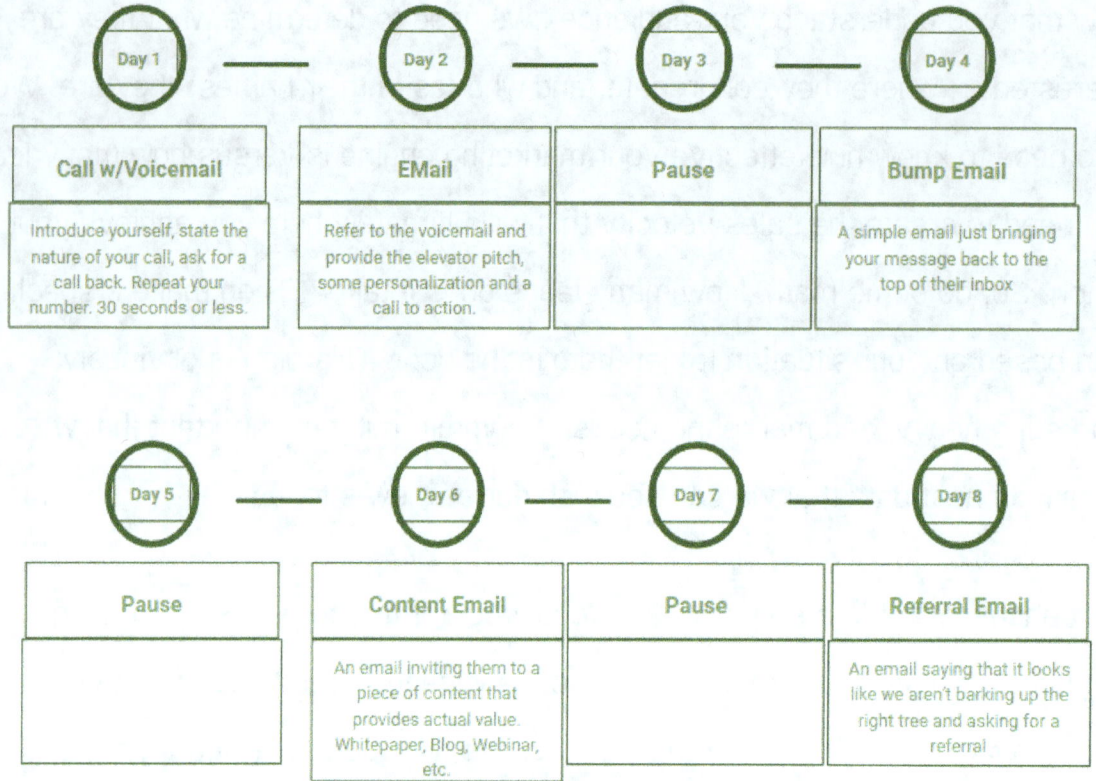

All of this can be easily managed by a sequencing tool that is part of or connected to your CRM. If you don't have a tool, you can do it manually with your calendar and tasks. I wouldn't recommend the manual approach unless you have an extremely small addressable market.

Once you have someone that is ready and able to meet, then it is time to take the next step!

Part 3D: Qualifying

What turns a lead into a prospect? How do we know? If you've nailed setting first appointments, this is a good opportunity for an improvement loop. For example, if a large proportion of the leads we are working could never be a buyer in spite of agreeing to a meeting, we need to revalue our lead sourcing and generation methodology. Beyond that, it is OK to start out with a fairly traditional qualification model. Is this someone we want to work with? Do they have a problem we can solve? Do they have or can they find the authority to spend the money? In a perfect world, would they like to solve that problem now? Document all of this with specific examples.

What do we need to work out before we call this an opportunity:
Is this someone that we may have business alignment with? Pretty simple. Are they a fit for our ICP? Yes, check! No. . .well, it depends. Mostly, we would ask for a referral. If they seem otherwise qualified, it might be a good idea to use this as another improvement loop. Is our ICP definition correct?
Do they have an explicit need that we can address? During the course of our initial conversation, we discovered that this person does, indeed, have a specific problem that our product or service can fix AND they are excited about what that means for their future state.
Do they have the authority to make this purchase? Right. Ask. In fact, find ways to ask this question in different ways very often. Note how many times the answer changes as we build trust.

Is it possible that they can find the funding to work with us? They can spend it, but do they have it? This isn't a "value" question at this point but, rather, the simple presence of money in the bank.

In a perfect world, would they like to get started in the near term? Timeline. "If this works out, would you like to start now? Yes!

Now, we have an opportunity!!

Part 4: Opportunity Process and Stages

Opportunity managment is compartmentalized, like a submarine. Close the door behind you before you open the one in front, or you will sink. It is OK to start with a simple model. In fact, simple is better. This is one place where none of us get points for creativity.

I was on the acquisition/transition leadership team for a specific type of software. They had hired a high dollar sales consultant to put together their sales process. It was, I kid you not, 10 stages long and had some really wild stages. For example, stage 2B was "Access to Power". This meant that before the rep could advance an opportunity past that stage, they had to actually speak to the ultimate decisionmaker. Well, as most anyone that has been selling for some time knows, it is a GREAT thing when you do get access to the ultimate decisionmaker, but it often never happens and we make the sale anyway. So, of their closed/won deals, fully 85% went from stage 2B to Stage 6A which was closed/won with none of the intermediate steps documented. Now, with your founder hat on, how in the heck can you forecast THAT? Or, even better, know what is going on in your pipeline at all? We are all much better off aligning our opportunity stages with naturally occurring events, sales process, and skill sets. This way, we can predict short term bookings, control our process and provide great coaching to our team. Let's go.

Stage 1: Baseline Qualified Opportunity

What we've worked out: per out qualifying stage above, we understand that there is a high probability that we want to work with this person/company and they have a good reason to work with us and, even better, they may have some money to do it with.

What we need to know: Which of our value drivers is most appealing to them? What are the specific reasons that not making the change will continue to cause them pain? What are the negative effects of that pain? What would the future state look like if that pain was gone?

Stage 2: Product Qualified

What we've worked out: They are excited to move forward, they are qualified per Stage 1, they are willing and able to provide customer deliverables to continue moving through the process.

What we need to know: through the process of deep discovery (part of the sales training plan), we need the customer to discover that the product/service will solve the problem that we are focused on with a high degree of confidence. We also need to know if they are willing and able to gather other key stakeholder that may influence the decision to get their buy-in as well.
Here's the question that we need an affirmative answer to: "Ms. Prospect, if you were to implement our ***, are you confident that it would lead you to the future state of *** that we discussed? Yes? Stage 3 it is!!

Stage 3. Finance qualified

What we know: Our prospect has made it this far, stakeholders are engaged and, sometimes, involved. Any follow up demonstrations or meetings further solidified the use case. The process is well underway.

What we need to find out: What is the purchasing process? Who is involved? How many steps? How long does it take? Is it agreed that the amount of money we are asking is commensurate with the value that they will realize. Is all of this information confirmed? Have we asked for any additional questions or objections? Is there any reason why we might not move forward? Have they agreed to review our terms/contract/agreement/quote/order form and/or shopping cart?

Stage 4: Verbal Agreement

What we know: We have confirmed everything. We have answered every objection. None of them are deal breakers. The customer has told us that they intend to buy and we've sent whatever documentation that we need in order to initiate the sale.

What we need to work out: Are their legal questions? Are the terms OK? When will they move forward?

Sometimes, at this step, a procurement team gets into the picture and wants to negotiate. If this happens with your product include a section on it in the playbook. For me, I don't negotiate with procurement. My champion has already agreed to the price. I also don't do government contracts or RFPs. If your business includes those, make sure to document your process. On that note, it is a dangerous thing to spend the opportunity cost of an RFP or lengthy procurement process in terms of a professional salesperson's time. The concentration of risk versus how many deals she could have closed with personally engaged customers can be enormous. Of course, some companies must do business this way. Just be aware of the tiger traps.

Stage 5: Closed/Won

What we know: We have a new client!
What we need to do: Deliver! Make them into screaming advocates! Celebrate!! and, make 5 more calls.

Stage 5a: Closed/Lost

We can get here from any stage. We lose anywhere from 30% to 80% of our deals depending on many variables. Closed/Lost is NOT a bad thing. We know we have to lose. We can always get better. Document what went wrong. Determine if it was a one off or something we should change either personally or in the process. Shake it off and . . . make 5 more calls.

Stage 6+: Post Sale Activities

Shipping, implementation, account management, customer engagement and/or a lot of things that are specific to you client journey. Put a placeholder here for whatever you need your dedicated sellers to do. Hand-Offs, evaluations, introductions, referral generation. . .anything. Just understand, the more non-selling activities that you assign to sellers, the less they will sell.

I've mentioned this before: Every good CRM has a way to manage opportunity stages. We'll insist that every step is documented and that the current deal stage is defensible for every opportunity. No guessing.

Part 5: Leadership Plan, The Simplified Version

So many sales leaders sit down with each rep, once a week, and grill them about when each deal in their pipeline is going to close. That is, in a word, dumb. Don't be dumb. It isn't leadership and it isn't even management. It is wishing. If you have the right process in place, your sales leader spends her time helping find ways to close more deals.

A. **Inspecting work**. This can be a manual motion or you can use tools like Interflexion, recorded meetings, and Gong! to provide insights. You MUST know what your people are saying, how prospects are responding, and what is being documented. You should NOT have to ask for this information. It is in the sales stack. If it is not, find out why. It is ok to repeat yourself here, but 100% adoption of documentation requirements is critical. If it isn't there, it didn't happen.

B. **Helping deals get across the finish line**. Or, as I like to call it, how 1:1s should work. Sit down with each rep once a week. Ask them how you can help, where they are stuck, or what questions they need answers to. Get into a rhythm. "I was looking at this opp and noticed something . did you explain this? Ask that?" Treat your sellers as if your livelihood depends on their success. It obviously does.

C. **Sales Meetings**. Similar to One on Ones, this is NOT a time to ask what deals are going to close when. You and/or your sales leaders already know this. You are well informed and ask questions in real time. Further, it is a waste of time to ask about status of deals in a group meeting. Group meetings have two distinct purposes. First, it is a chance for to provide updates to what's happening in the company. Product updates, finance updates, staff changes, etc. Having a culture of transparency is critical. Answer questions honestly. This team is the reason the company is growing, if you can't trust them, you hired the wrong people. Second, the weekly team meeting is the best time to do group training and discussions that are "ripped from the headlines". In other words, when you are inspecting sales calls, there will always be trends; common objections and many making the same errors are examples. Use the time to talk through what's happening and come up with solutions. Again, the job of the leader is to HELP the sales team succeed. It is NOT to whip them into submission publicly. You, as a leader, might very well be panicked, but the second you transfer that panic to the sales team; you are on a downward spiral to the bottom. Always provide value.

D. **Upstream and downstream KPIs**. In my favorite model, it is all about conversion metrics. How many of "this" does it take to make a "that"? Create individual benchmarks and team goals that all roll back up to the vision. Activity metrics only become important if something is broken. A person isn't doing their job, the product doesn't provide value.

D. **Forecasting**. Based on C, above, what does our velocity look like, does it get us to our vision and, if not, what needs to change to get us there? It is JUST MATH. Everyone should understand that the commonality in all sales forecasting is that it is always wrong. Constantly adjust to get as close to right as possible. You and your exec team can make better decisions with a clearer crystal ball.

E. **Onboarding**. Make a specific action plan on getting new reps up to speed and having sales conversations quickly. The very best way to do this is through repeated exposure, practice and feedback. They don't need to know everything about the product at first (PLEASE GET THAT). They do need to know how the product helps your customers and the common objections they may encounter. They also need to know (if they are an AE/Sales Rep) how to pitch the product. Include sections on documentation/sales operation. System training and, of course, training on the playbook. It should be about 80% self study and 20% meetings and feedback. I love tools like Interflexion and Gong! to provide practice and inspect progress. Just an aside, but live role play is a tough one. Using either a simulated environment or live fire is better. Yes, you will be burning some leads, but that is the cost of onboarding.

F. **Offboarding**. As an absolute last result when it is doing a human, the team, and the company a disservice to have them on the team, it is important to have a professional, empathetic offboarding plan. Work with whoever you use for HR to devise this BEFORE you have to use it. This is the worst part of the sales leader's job. The proper way to frame it is that you made a mistake. You made the bad decision to hire someone that wasn't able to align with the team. As such, it is your responsibility as a human being and a leader to escort that person off the team. Even if you are in an "at will" employment situation, it is important to provide context for the termination and resources. When does this not apply? Bad actors. If someone does something genuinely bad, there are no second chances. The team needs to understand that their leaders have their back at all times. We cannot allow bad behavior. Zero tolerance.

G. **Promotion/Relegation**. Put together a plan that provides a solid career path for your team. In sales, it should be 90% objective and 10% culture. Reason: if someone is on the team, they should always be a good culture fit, but if they are being promoted, they should be a role model. So, the plan looks like this: If you do this, you get that. For example: if a sales rep has six month tenure and has exceeded their quota for the last 3 months, they are promoted from SR1 to SR2. This includes an increase in On Target Earnings (OTE, discussed later). For relegation (demotion), the rule needs to allow for "life" and market events so, it should be harder to be demoted. In the scenario above, it could be "If an SR2 has less than 85% of quota for 4 consecutive months, they are considered for relegation to SR1." The last thing anyone wants is for a team member to be so well fed that they become complacent.

H. **Compensation structure**. This is the age old problem. It can be structured many ways. Here are the basics of what has worked well. Use the idea of On Target Earnings (OTE). Meaning, if someone on the team meets 100% of their quota, they earn a total of 100% of their target. Now, if you are a start up, you need to make sure that each rep is profitable at about 85% of their OTE. Normally, that means that they have to provide about 4 times 85% (3.4 times) of their OTE in gross margin. If you sell software or other things that are based in vapor, it may be easier to use 5 times revenue. This is a guideline. Typically, your compensation structure will gain efficiency as people get better and make more money. It is 100% desirable to have a sales person be the highest paid person in the company provided that their compensation plan is designed to provide ROI across the board. Do NOT change compensation structures if people start to make too much money (what does that even mean?). When it comes to sales people, the more money they make, the more money you make. Give them the opportunity to get wealthy. Right? RIGHT!

Within the compensation structure, it is important to also specify how your team members are rewarded for going above and beyond. Of course, you will have things like spiffs and bonuses, but beyond that; how do you recognize someone both publicly and privately for doing an amazing job. Encourage other leaders to set up a similar structure for their teams. Also, it is important to note that not everyone loves to be singled out in public. Introverts think it is punishment. Now, there aren't many introverts in sales, but they are there. Make sure you are sensitive to everyone's communication language.

I. **Lead Ownership and Conflict De-escalation**. These two concepts are in the same category because lead ownership will be your biggest source of conflict, right up until it isn't. Let me explain. You have a hand open, abundance mentality when it comes to your culture around leads. There must be enough to go around. If not, then you are likely in the wrong space. Hard truth. That stated, there will still be times that more than one person has, in their minds, a legitimate claim to the same lead. The process here is quite simple. They, as grown ass adults, should have a conversation about who has the best chance of closing the deal and where the lead came from. For example, if an AE's cousin signs up for a demo without telling the AE and it is assigned in the round robin, that AE should provide assistance, but they did a bad job of prospecting so the deal stays with the assignee from the round robin. The inverse is also true. For example, if a sales rep is actively working a deal and someone from that same company signs up for a sales consultation with a different email address and, as such, is assigned to a different rep. The original rep has claim. If the right outcome can't be agreed upon, it is escalated to leadership. The leader can assign the lead to whomever they see fit. It could even be to a third person. Sometimes, that is a good idea because creating a shark tank is a great way to kill a good team!

Now, a couple of tiny pieces of leadership guidance.

First, trust your team. Yes, that keeps coming up. A former CEO that I worked with extensively said, "The key to leadership is to hire brilliant people, involve them in goal setting and then get the Hell out of the way."

Second, be transparent. Unless something is highly confidential like compensation or mergers and acquisition info that isn't solid yet, err on the side of transparency. That will go a long ways to make your team trust you and be more intentional rather than speculative (see the bonus content section for more on that).

Third, be one of them but not one of them. Impossible, right? Well, it is difficult buy you need to be able to show them that you have the chops to do what they do. Pick up the phone, make a few sales calls with them. Let them see you fail. Be their advocate, but treat them all the same. Every single person on the team should know that you have their back 100% of the time as long as they are doing the things they need to do.

Forth, the team as its own organism needs to look to you as its head. The body must trust the decisions made by the head. The buck stops with you. Your locus of control has to be so strong that there is never any questions that you speak for the company. You make the companies mistakes. You do not I disparage anyone in the company at any time, even if they desperately deserve it. You address concerns in public and let the fur fly in private. You are the alpha wolf that is in charge of protecting the growth engine.

Fifth, and conversely, there is NO tolerance for anyone attacking your team. Constructive feedback is always welcome but sales people are kind of unique in that they have to both love people and be OK with constant rejection. It is your job to deliver corrective action an no one else'. If your pack trusts you, they will come to work for you on days that they don't feel up to it. Stand up. Be their rock.

Even with a small team, the sales leader's job is nearly infinite even though it is just a few things. A few very challenging things that can make your company soar if she is giving the right tools and people.

Part: The Last Part

We've just been outline how to do your first sales playbook. There are certainly company and industry specific gaps that need to be filled. No question. There are also a ton of other things to be address that could be included but are also ripe for other plans. These include onboarding, recruiting, ongoing training, commission structures, promotion levels, job descriptions and much, much more. But, let's eat this elephant one bit at a time.

Always default back to:

What do we sell?

Who do we sell it to?

How does it help them?

How do we track progress?

YOU can do this. Even if you need a little help!

NOTE: I didn't suggest starting with a sales operations plan. You should be able to start selling now. With a solid sales plan, you can fill in the gaps in the tech stack later. It is the same old story: Process, People, Systems. They are all dynamic and all important, but don't let one stop you from the others.

Bonus Content: Change Management

Big changes are coming. It is inevitable. In this case, you are implementing a disruptive process that insists people document every conversation. That's a big deal and can be upsetting to some.

How do you prepare yourself and your team for the transition to the new normal? There are certainly volumes of books, blogs, vlogs and podcasts on this topic and many of them offer sound advice. My perspective strips it down to the essence of what drives resistance to change and flips the script to make every big shift positive for our high performing team. Caution: this simply doesn't work for people that are currently working just hard enough not to get fired or that we are paying just enough so they won't quit. You'll see why.

A few years ago, I was leading the sales team for a rapidly growing startup. We were outpacing the growth of our nearest competitors by four to five times. It was EXCITING. Over the previous couple of years, we had gone from a team of 3 to 7 to 12 to 40 high performing team members. We were segmenting our ICP and specializing our roles. Then, the other shoe dropped.

We had done so well and grown so fast that our little privately held company was being sold to a larger organization that was, in turn, owned by private equity. Oh my goodness, what was to happen next??

Well, long story. Short version. We did what was affectionately called a "reverse acquisition". Our sales team took over the sales and marketing function for all of the software divisions of the company that bought us. We absorbed their team, applied our processes, and lost ZERO people from our team. Zero.

How? That's the big question. When the announcement leaked (there is always a leak), speculation was certainly afoot. People were wondering what the future held for them as individuals first and, second, as an organization. The new company was a competitor. It was larger. It looked lean and mean. Meanwhile, we were the Battlestar Galactica of teams. The Rag-Tag Fugitive Fleet. At least on the surface. In fact, we had solid processes, great front line leaders, solid recruiting, and a vision-driven battle cry. We'd certainly lost battles, but we were the clear leaders in the war. But, still, change scares the f**k out of people.

Here's how we made it happen. **We replaced speculation with intention.** Period. The end. That's all. Humans have two powerful ways to look at the future. Speculation assumes we have no control. People that speculate daily have a low locus of control (another whole book). On the other hand, people that look to the future with intention believe that they are in control of their own destinies. But, big changes will shake the foundations of even the most intentional humans.

First, I met with the team in an informal setting on one of our sales floors. We just gathered in a huddle. We acknowledged that the change was coming. I promised to be as absolutely transparent about what was happening as possible and then, I asked a simple question:

"What do you want to happen? We know that the change is coming and within that system, what do you intend?" As long as it was within the realm of possibility, we set goals and made plans to focus solely on these intentions. Then we went to work. Magic ensued. **PURE MAGIC.** Records were broken, leaders emerged and we, as a team, won the war together.

Intention is a rocket motor, speculation is an anchor.

What's next?

You have created this beautiful, dynamic sales process and want to implement it! Great! Go for it! However, it is critical to do a few things.

Thing 1: Get your sales operations plan in order. What software and resources will your team use to execute and document EVERYTHING. This can include but it is not limited to CRM, video conferencing, sales training tools, feedback tools, instant messaging, sales acceleration, sales enablement, reporting engines, etc. Start with what you have today and then fill in the gaps as the become problems. Don't solve for problems you don't have.

Thing 2: People. Get the right people on this trip with you. Hire for character, grit and (maybe) experience. Do not expect sales people to survive on their own. As of this edition (2024), I still see companies hiring sales people with no experience, training, leadership or real idea of what success looks like. Once you have great humans, they need to be nurtured.

Thing 3: Create an in depth training plan that is 75% sales and communications with the remaining 25% process and product. Most companies do the opposite. If you teach people to communicate, they can sell anything. Your product will change. I like to call this "proactive change management". Prepare people for everything and they'll be ready for anything.

So, we're not done quite yet, but we are ready to begin filling in the blanks!
Let's GO!!!

Appendix: Sample Sales Playbook

If you would like a copy of this in either PowerPoint or Google Slides, send me an email at jmoss@inertiasolutions.io. Free of charge!

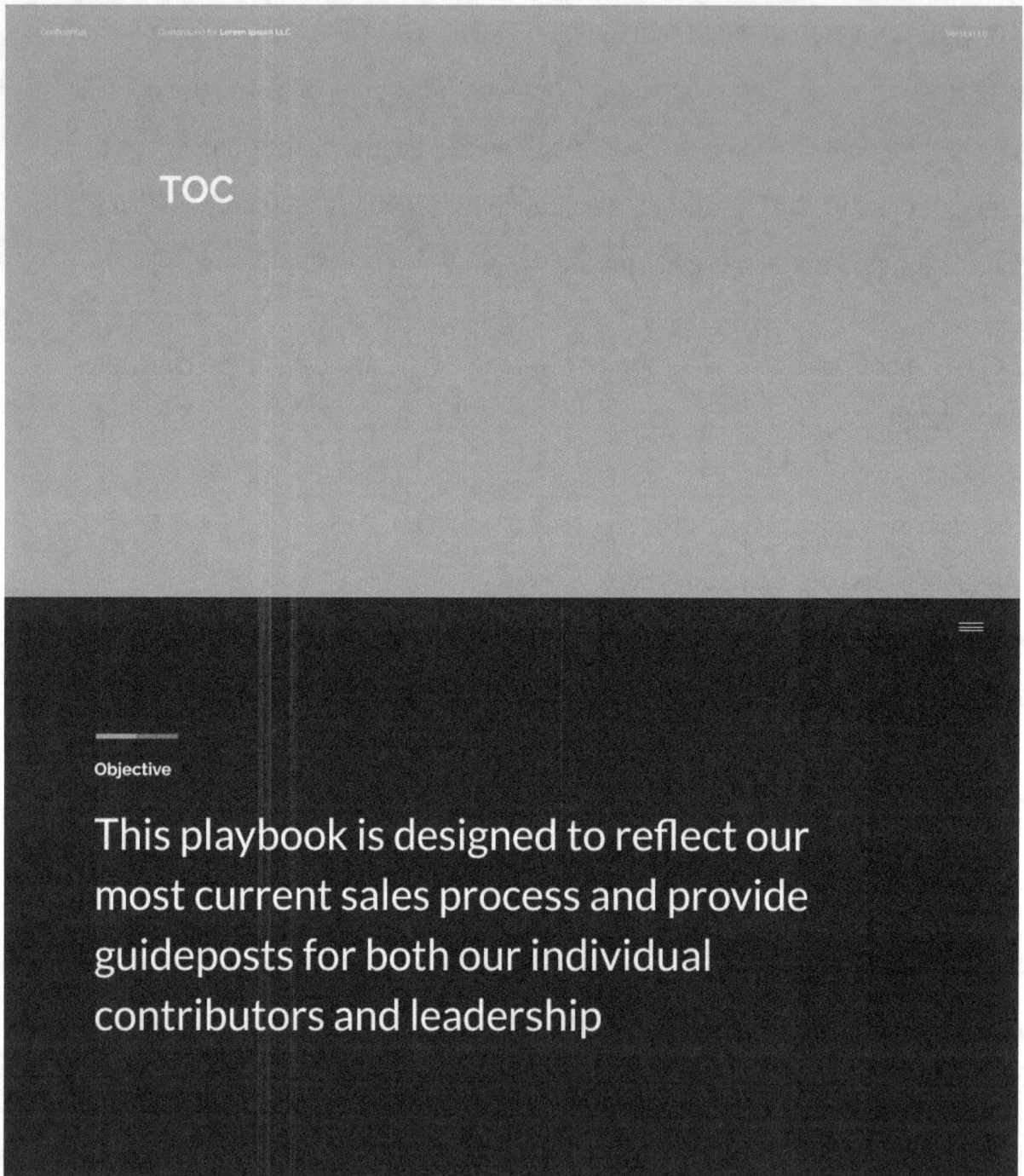

TOC

Objective

This playbook is designed to reflect our most current sales process and provide guideposts for both our individual contributors and leadership

Foundations

Vision

To become . . .

HINT: DO NOT SKIP THIS. If you don't have the authority to create a company vision, then create one for your area of influence. Sales, Sales and Marketing, Sales and Customer Success...etc.

Mission

We exist to…

Leadership Brand

How we behave…

Expectations for all

1. You have the authority to make decisions. We believe in you and trust you.
2. Every lead/prospect/customer interaction is documented thoroughly in the CRM. This is NOT optional.
3. All inbound leads will be contacted in as close to real time as possible. Our standard is under 5 minutes during business hours.
    a. If they have provided a phone number, we call first.
4. We have abundance mentality. There are plenty of leads for everyone. As a rule, we don't have lead conflict.
5. We provide clear, concise, balanced feedback to everyone inside the company that we interact with.
6. We strive to get better every day.
7. This playbook will be revalued often and evolve. Your feedback is important.

Main Value Drivers (What Out Customers Need)

1. Efficiency:

3. Engagement:

2. Speed:

4. Profit:

HINT: These are the things that your customers tell you are the reasons that they buy from you. The categories are placeholders. Be specific.

Ideal Customer Profile

Our ideal customer is a ***** who works for a ***** in the capacity of *****.

They are frustrated by ***** and need to *****. If they don't ****, it means that *****.

If they DO *****, they will gain *****

Buyer Personas

1.
2.
3.

HINT: It is OK to have more than 3, but your salespeople need to have focus. You can also duplicate this page for each persona rather than having them all on one. More detail is better.

Insert pictures that represent you buyers

Lead Generation

Where Our Leads Come From

1. Advertising: (MQLs from SEM, print ads, radio ads, any ads that the marketing team PAYs for. Define those here.)
2. Content: (MQLs from your expertise; content on your website, people that read your book, white papers, conference presentations, blogs, vlogs, podcasts, etc)
3. Intelligent Outreach: People that we truly believe should be customers but don't know about us yet.
4. Referrals.

QUICK TIP

Try right clicking on a photo and using "Replace Image" to show your own photo.

Hint: Narrow this down to what applies to you and clearly define each channel. Leads from partners/resellers/etc. Can either be considered referrals or have their own playbook if they are a big part of your strategy.

Sales Development Process

Option 1: Sales Development (Qualifying leads and establishing an open line of 2 way communications) as a specialized function (The SDR/BDR model).

Option 2: Sales Reps (Account Executives) have the responsibility of developing their own leads.

Option 3: Hybrid. Typically, sales reps will develop leads provided by marketing while sales development reps will be responsible for outreach.

HINT: Define who is responsible for what here. Many times, companies will start with sales reps doing it all and then make the change later.

Lead Ownership and Conflict Resolution

1. How we clear leads in the CRM
2. Criteria for lead ownership (for example, 2 way contact within 6 months or recent assignment may establish ownership)
3. Conflict resolution process
    a. Talk it out based on who has the best chance of advancing the deal.
    b. Take it to leadership if agreement can't be reached.
    c. Clearly state that all leads are company leads

Lead Processing

1. How you handle sales development operations (CRM, Sequencing Tool, Email tool, Lead Enrichment tool, etc.
2. Customized sequence management (how do your buyers like to be contacted? What types of messaging appeal to their value drivers, etc.)
3. Link to the folder/location with your sequences
4. Outreach customization process.
5. Guidelines on how many new leads should be placed in sequence each day.
6. Best practices/examples
7. Definitions of what qualifies a lead to move on to the sale process.

Sample Sequences

Cold/Outbound Sequence format

Hint: This is probably 4 or 5 slides.

Sample Sequences

MQL Sequence format

Hint: This is probably 4 or 5 slides.

Content Sequence format

Sample Sequences

Hint: This is probably 4 or 5 slides.

Qualified-Bad Timing Sequence format

Sample Sequences

Hint: This is probably 4 or 5 slides.

Sales Development to Sales Handoff Process

Suggestions to get you started

1. SDR qualifies the lead and sets the meeting on the sales rep's calendar and performs all confirmation steps.
2. SDR "owns" the lead until the lead shows up to the sales rep's initial discovery/demo meeting.
    a. If the lead is a no-show, the SDR hunts them down.
3. SDR transfers ownership to sales rep

HINT: Only applicable if you choose to separate the sales development and sales roles

Sales Stages

Sales Process Stage 1: Qualified Prospect

1. Do we have an opportunity? (Part 3D)
   a. What we know
   b. What we need to work out
2. If Yes, an opportunity/deal is opened in the CRM. Err on the side of opening more so we can see why we lose.

IF you have a very complex product, this is usually where sales engineers or solutions architects come in. They should have their own process, but this is a good place to document the interaction with the sales rep.

Suggestion: The sales rep should own the interaction with the sales engineer, but should defer to the sales engineer as the expert on the product.

Sales Process Stage 2: Product Qualified

1. Does the prospect agree that our product fulfills their need?
2. What we know
3. What we need to work out

Sales Process Stage 2: Product Qualified Part 2 (optional)

Sales Engineering Plan

Do you need sales engineering? Does that happen inside your sales team? Is it in your customer success, implementation or product teams?

This is a wildly variable topic that typically only applies to very complex products like expensive medical equipment and complex software.

Sales Process Stage 4: Verbal Approval

1. All stakeholders have agreed that, when details are agreed upon, they will be making purchase?
2. What we know
3. What we need to work out

Sales Process Stage 5: Closed/Won

1. We have sent an invoice and/or received final authorization to fulfill the order
2. What we know
3. What we need to work out

Sales Process Stage 5a: Closed/Lost

1. In spite of doing everything we could, we had to stop moving forward with this prospect.
2. Why didn't they buy?
3. What did we learn?
    a. Provide feedback where needed
4. Is there hope?

Sales Process Stage 6+ Post Sales 1

Short term responsibilities once the deal is closed

Hand off, implementation, fulfillment, initial customer feedback, etc.

Sales Process
Stage 6+
Post Sales 2

Long term post sales responsibilities

Account management (This is a completely different playbook, but it needs to be mentioned and linked)

Long term follow up/progress points

Referral generation

Leadership

Sales Leadership Process: Inspecting Work

1. What to look for?
    a. Effective communication
    b. Complete documentation
    c. Product knowledge
    d. Much more
2. Where to look?
    a. CRM
    b. Sales enablement tool
    c. Dashboards

Sales Leadership Process: 1 on 1

1. 1 on 1s
    a. Outline
    b. Lead from the front
    c. Always about helping sales reps be better
    d. Seek feedback

Sales Leadership Process: Coaching

1. Side by Side coaching
    a. Providing thoughtful, balanced feedback.
    b. Tools you use.
    c. Frequency
    d. Coaching outline

Sales Leadership Process: Sales Meetings

1. Team Training Meetings
    a. Frequency
    b. Length
    c. Content
        i. Company Updates
        ii. Sales Training

Sales Leadership Process: KPIs

Hint: If it makes sense, consider outsourcing sales operations or hiring a manager of sales ops when the metrics get too deep

1. What are they? Examples:
   a. Key conversion metrics
      i. Lead to Prospect
      ii. Prospect to Customer
      iii. Drill down
         1. Stage 1 to Stage 2
         2. Stage 2 to Stage 3
         3. Etc.
         4. Sales Rep v. Benchmark
         5. Lead types v. Benchmark
         6. Sequence 1 v. Sequence 2
      iv. Average Contract Value
      v. Deal Cycle
         1. How long to win
         2. How long to lose
   b. Where do they live?
      i. Dashboards
         1. Management
         2. Team
         3. Individual

Sales Leadership Process: Forecasting

Hint: If it makes sense, consider outsourcing sales operations or hiring a manager of sales ops when the metrics get too deep

1. What is the model?
   a. How far out can you predict?
   b. Can you see problems before they occur?
2. Develop a dynamic model
   a. Sales Velocity
   b. Conversions v. Sales Cycle v. number of leads
      i. By type, size, vertical, everything

Sales Leadership Process: Executive Reporting

Executive Reporting:

What reports and feedback go to the exec meeting and the frequency of their updates.

Sales Leadership Process: Recruiting

Recruiting Plan

Sales Leadership Process: Promotion

If you do this, you get that...

Expectations

Sales Leadership Process: Relegation

If you don't do this, you get that taken away

Sales Leadership Process: Onboarding

Onboarding Plan

Sales Leadership Process: Off-Boarding

Empathetic and Compassionate Off-Boarding plan

Sales Leadership Process: Commission Structure

Overview and details of how commissions are built.

HINT: Don't do custom commission structure per rep.

Sales Leadership Process: Recognition

Thoroughly document how you recognize top performers and heroes.

1. Private feedback
2. Public praise
3. Spiffs
4. Bonuses
5. President's club

HINT: Don't do custom commission structure per rep.

Other Stuff

Sales Leadership Process: Interdepartmental Collaboration

Things like
Sale engineering/solutions architecture

Product 360 feedback

Issues that cause us to lose sales

Implementation

Customer service

Sales Leadership Process: Leadership Brand

Refer back to the leader's responsibility to the vision.

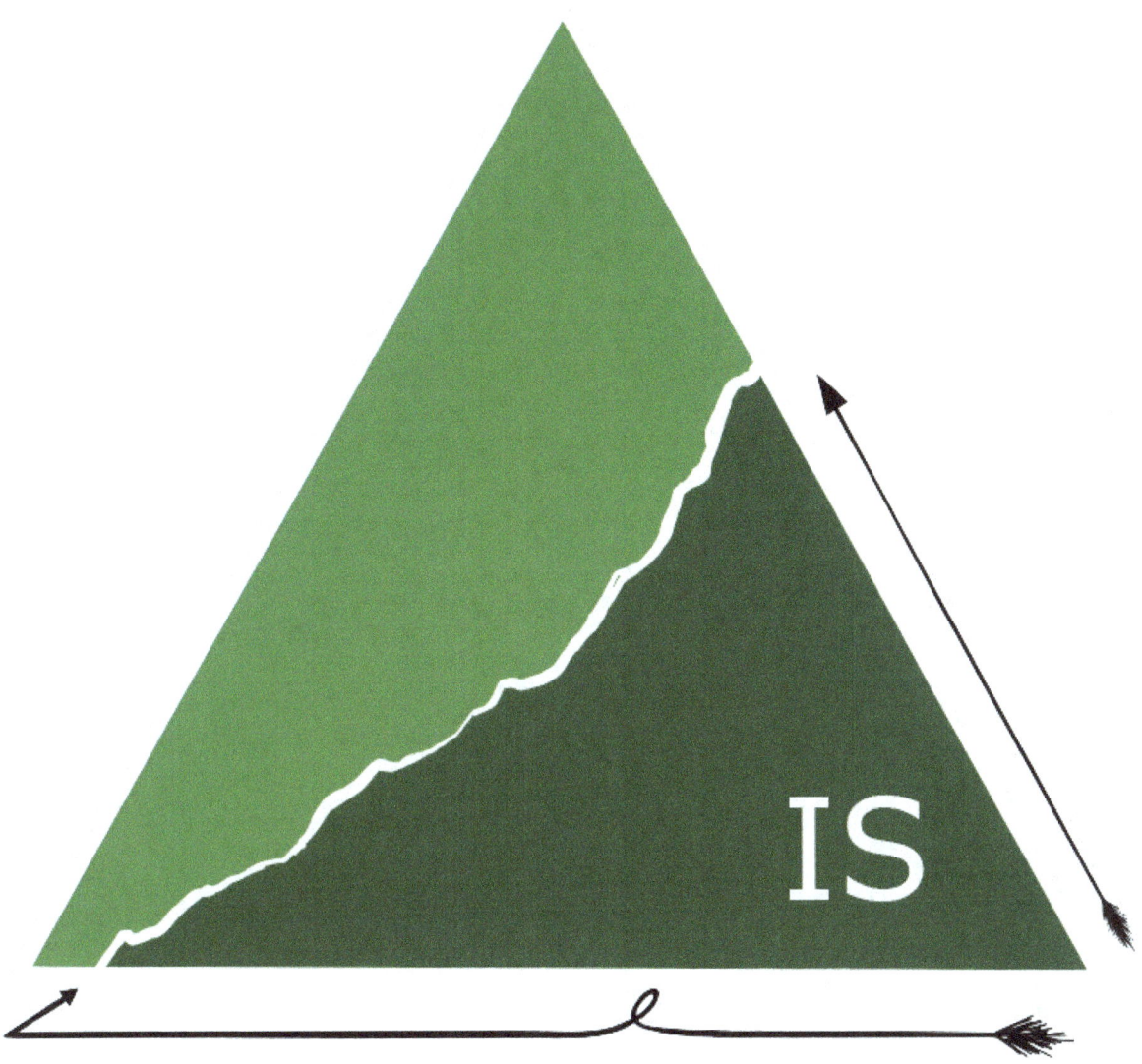

Thanking a few people:

Of course, thanks to my family for their support and faith.

Especially Lori. You've been the reason for all I do. Forever.

Sara. Inertia Solutions wouldn't exist without you. You have my gratitude and my friendship for life. Thank you so much for helping to get this snowball rolling.

www.ingramcontent.com/pod-product-compliance
Lightning Source LLC
Chambersburg PA
CBHW062227220526

45471CB00009B/3383